P

S ... *The Nature*

...ook of the

LONGLISTED: Wainwright Prize for Nature Writing, *The Nature of Autumn*

BBC RADIO 4 BOOK OF THE WEEK, *The Nature of Spring*

"Crumley has a great gift for observation." Kathleen Jamie

"The best guide I know to the natural world." Malachy Tallach

"Scotland's pre-eminent nature writer." *Guardian*

"Enthralling and often strident." *The Observer*

"Well-written…elegant." *Times* "An exceptional and intense quality of observation glows from every page … Nothing can diminish the sharpness of his eye." Joyce McMillan, *The Scotsman*

"A mesmerising blend of observation and in-depth knowledge about our wild landscapes." *The Herald*

"Effortlessly captures the majesty … The perfect finale to this evocative seasonal collection." *BBC Wildlife Magazine*

"Compelling … Radical … He could be Ali Smith's naturalist twin." *Scottish Review of Books*

Hare

ENCOUNTERS IN THE WILD

Jim Crumley

Saraband

Published by Saraband
3 Clairmont Gardens
Glasgow, G3 7LW

www.saraband.net

ISBN: 9781916812659

Printed and bound in Great Britain by Clays Ltd, Elcograf S.p.A.

1 2 3 4 5 6 7 8 9

MIX
Paper | Supporting responsible forestry
FSC® C018072

"All good things are wild and free."

Henry David Thoreau

ONE

THE BADGER was in the brown hare's field, or perhaps it was the other way round. Or perhaps neither hare nor badger felt possessive about the field at all, and it was just another field, a source of earthworms for a badger, a source of grass for a hare. And although it certainly was not my field, to me it was a source of badgers and hares. And lapwings. And skylarks. And now that I think about it (and in no particular order of significance or season or anything else), a source of yellowhammers, field mice, field voles, moles, hedgehogs, roe deer, fox; pink-footed geese, mute swans and whooper swans; hunting buzzards, kestrels, owls (various), merlin (one). And once there was a feeding flock of 300 bramblings. Oh, and grey partridges, and the sparrowhawks that ambushed them along by the hedge, first severing then discarding their heads while the bodies were still warm and twitchy. That way, I found three partridge heads and one headless body by the hedge in one week of one winter.

But mostly when I think of that field I think of the badger and the hare. I was trying to discover where badgers went when they left the sett. Like watching birds at the nest, watching badgers at the sett only tells you so much. I wanted to meet them walking the badger paths of their territory, and after a great many night shifts I established that one badger made a habit of ducking under the fence at the edge of the field in question, then crossed the field, stopping often to dig up worms, before leaving the field by ducking under the fence on the opposite side of the field, the sparrowhawk side. So I reasoned the badger would come back the same way it had gone, which is why I was sitting on top of a small bank above the path where it entered the field. I was waiting for the badger to come back. I was still waiting when I saw the hare.

She (I knew she was a "she" by this time, but the badger was still an "it") came up the field from the direction of the firth at a gentle lope, canted forward as if she sought out some fundamental principle of aerodynamics so that she moved more smoothly and efficiently, but in reality because her hind legs are longer than her front legs and her hind feet are twice the size of her front feet. She held her ears tall and they scanned the night restlessly, and unlike a badger on the move (direct and purposeful), she looked lost and uncertain. Her line wavered. Once she doubled back for about twenty yards, made a startling leap several yards sideways, then U-turned again so that she began to come up the field again, but further out from the fence.

She obsesses about her scent trail. This is her way of confusing the enemy, especially if she is on her way back to her form (a temporary refuge, nothing more than a shallow scrape or a hidden patch of flattened grass where she lies low, and where she has her leverets, and – most of the time – leaves them alone to work things out for themselves). Right there and right then, and for the first time, I made a connection between hare and badger: does she equate the badger with her idea of "the enemy" as well as the more obvious fox and the glaringly obvious man with a gun? And then I thought of one good reason why she might: had she made her form close to where the badger path negotiated the fence, and might there be leverets in it? In which case, however you choose to look at it, the badger was in the hare's field, trespassing with menace.

* * *

It was late evening, the end of April. A ground mist hung about in loose strands. The sky was pale in the north, the firth bounced the last of the daylight across the tilted plain of the field, and the moon was on the rise just behind the treetops so that huge tree-shadows patterned the field almost all the way across. Considering this was West Lothian and a dozen miles from Edinburgh, there was an undeniable pastel beauty about the way the night approached the land.

The hare had stopped. She sat back, studied them both – the night and the land. She had the best nose, the best eyes and demonstrably the best ears in all that landscape, but I have many moons of practising the arts of silence and stillness under my belt, and given the windlessness of the night she would have to be very close to catch my scent. Besides, suddenly she had the distraction of company. The thick grass at the field's edge first began to waver then parted and three blunt-headed leverets just days old and inches long crawled none too certainly towards her. She bent to lick them one by one, and they fumbled and stumbled into her to suckle where she sat. I had never seen this before and I was oddly moved by something in the elemental simplicity of the sight. Then we – the hare and I – heard the fence on the far side of the field twang softly.

The hare's ears twitched and her head turned slightly, not to face the sound directly, but certainly to comb the darkness. Her eyes protrude like glass beads from the outsides of the widest part of her skull, like a woodcock's, so she has, as near as makes no difference, 360-degree vision.

But when she wants to look directly at something she looks at it side-headed and through one eye. At times like that, when I have been the subject of hare scrutiny, I always wonder what the other eye is looking at, wonder if she can focus both eyes independently and simultaneously so that at any one moment she carries in her head a clear picture of what is going on all around her in every direction.

In that so-utter stillness, then, we had both heard the quiet response of the fence to some animal movement or other. I understood its meaning because six or seven nights in the last dozen I had sat here, shadowed and still on the bank, when a badger head-butted the bottom strand of the fence on this side of the field, squeezed underneath, and stepped into the field, the fence restoring itself with just that very noise, that quiet, complaining twang. No matter that on these other nights I had been sitting only ten feet away from the source of that sound, and the fence the hare and I had just heard was seventy or eighty yards away, there was no mistaking its meaning in my mind even for an instant.

I shifted my binoculars from the hare to the far side of the field, focussing on the black outline of the head-high hedge that bounded it. That was my first movement since the hare had turned up, and if she had been unaware of my presence before, she was unaware no longer. In the same instant, my binoculars confirmed that the badger was in the hare's field. So within the space of one or two seconds the hare heard the fence, understood its meaning, saw me, and saw and scented the badger. She also had three newborns obliviously tucked into her maternal bodily warmth. It was one of her life's trickier moments.

Meanwhile, the badger was crossing the field, going home, and if it followed the pattern of all the other nights I had sat here, it would duck under the fence ten feet from me and twenty yards from the hare. But sooner or later it was bound to discover the distraction of the hare and the succulent appeal of helpless leverets. The badger is an omnivore, prefers earthworms to anything else, but would not be averse to a few mouthfuls of unjugged hare. I watched it plod rhythmically out into the middle of the field, the white stripes of its head accentuating the carthorse-like nod at every stride, its legs mimicking the bear's in-swinging gait. But the badger does not have the hare's eyes, and sometimes (say on a night of shifting eye-level mists and the immense moonshadows of the big trees) its eyesight lets it down. Its ears are good, however, and its nose is exceptional. But at this time of their lives leverets have one unique quality in their favour – a complete absence of scent.

The hare acted. First she bundled the leverets into the long grass at the field's edge, where they simply flattened, lay still, and vanished from sight. One thing hares of all ages understand is the worth of stone-stillness.

Then the hare was out in the field, heading off the badger by drawing its attention. By now the badger had stopped and was paying close attention to movement and sound and the blatant scent of the adult hare, and in the badger's mind the most certain factor was that the hare was nursing and that somewhere nearby were leverets, and that most-likely somewhere was surely in the long grass at the field edge. So the badger changed direction and moved off past the hare as if she wasn't there, following its nose down the trail the hare had just left.

Badgers go out of their way to avoid confrontation. They will turn the other cheek before they get involved in a fight, but it is also fair to say that if they do get involved they usually win. The chances are that the hare knew that, but her maternal instincts outpaced her innate caution, and the badger was only a few yards and not many seconds away from discovering – and almost certainly devouring – her young. As the badger walked past her, almost pushing her aside, she turned her back on it and lashed out backwards with both hind feet. The badger was caught squarely amidships and I heard the soft, dull thud and the gasp as the badger was knocked a yard sideways and landed on its back. It was not the biggest badger I have ever seen but nor was it particularly small, and even a small one weighs more than twenty pounds; I would guess the hare had just turned more than thirty pounds of badger upside down.

It lay there for a few seconds, quite still, then stood and shook itself and looked round. It was at that point that I realised the hare was not in sight, and neither I nor the badger had seen it go. The badger turned away south up the field's steepening, darkening slope and disappeared into tree shadows and ground mist and nightfall.

* * *

Sometimes stillness is everything. The temptation after such a startling, climactic moment is to call it a night. What can follow that? What more can the night possibly have to offer? But the other side of that particular temptation is a different question, and now I asked it of myself: what makes you think the hare is done with the night just because she kicked a badger in the ribs? Besides, I was perfectly placed if she was not done with the night, I didn't have to move, and sometimes stillness is everything. So I sat still and waited. An hour drifted away, a slow hour that left midnight behind. No badger, no leverets, no hare.

The badger's point of entry and exit to and from the field was at the end of an old loan, a long, narrow belt of big trees that ran along a crest between fields. The badger's path crept along its centre, half-hidden by mostly un-grazed grass, although fox and roe deer stepped that way, as did I on many an unsleeping night, as did most of the small furry clan of farmland-woodland creatures on their stop-start travels between traumas such as owl-call, hawk-fall, badger-prowl, and the earth-trembling imminence of size nine wellies. This path ended at the fence, beyond which lay the field of the badger-kicking hare.

The fence was new and ran the whole length of the field; the hedge that ran just inside it was old. There was a gap in the hedge where the end of the loan met the field. The gap was why the badger crossed there. Whatever the reason for it, I appreciated it, for it gave me a broad sightline into the field. And it was through that hedge that the hare and leverets had probably disappeared. Perhaps she could have moved them far down the field. Hares often move their young after one of life's many alarms, or just to keep their enemies guessing. Leverets are born fully furred and with their eyes open, and possessing a lifelong sense of independence that seems to kick in from day one.

Or, the hare may have just hunkered down in the moon-deepened shadows of the dark side of the hedge, low to the ground, ears flattened along her spine, teaching the leverets by example their first lesson in the art of hare-stillness.

* * *

The moon climbed high above the trees beyond the far side of the field, contriving a night of raw, primitive beauty out of the still-lingering wisps of mist, the pale, tumbling curves of field, the parallel inked-in blue-black curves of the hedges, the quiet and surprisingly pale shades of the distant firth. Lapwings sighed in a fold of the field, soft, lilting contact calls so that the flock maintained an illusion of vigilance even as it dozed away the high-tide hours. Tawny owls stabbed at the darkness with sharp, two-syllable shrieks, or else they layered it with creamy, churring croons. Then there was a hare, far down the field.

It ran easily out into the moonlight from the hedge on the far side and at once it was partnered in dance by its own giant shadow. Then there were hares running towards it from a dozen different parts of the field edge, and for several minutes they ran interweaving lines and haphazard circles around each other in a loose and apparently shapeless choreography of companionship. It seemed to have no other purpose, for it soon ran out of momentum and slowly the animals separated and settled into a space of their own to feed.

I had been vaguely aware for a while of a soft rustling from just beyond the end of the gap in the hedge where the shadows lay deepest, as if an errant and determined breeze was at work. But I was so absorbed in the spectacle of the hares that I let it rustle on unquestioned. I now questioned it. *Was* it the wind? But the night was windless. I turned my head towards the sound. The hedge was twitching. Then the long grass began to whisper and something like a periscope moved slowly there; two periscopes – the raised ears of the badger-kicker. She inched out into the edge of the field where the moon found her and she froze under its cold stare. She sat up, she raised her front feet off the ground, she studied the field, she studied the air, she listened and listened. She moved a yard and the leverets tumbled out after her, grouped in a tight arch around her tail. They copied her every action. When she set off at an easy jog they trooped behind her in single file. Minutes later they were embraced by the gathering of their own kind. The night was hers and she had earned it by right.

TWO

FLANDERS Moss is a raised bog, a wide-open and flat sprawl of land between the fields of the Carse of Stirling (the broad river valley of the upper Forth) and the foothills of the southernmost Highlands. From west to north an arc of mountains astounds, especially in winter with their snows and their bruise-coloured sunsets, and in early summer when they rise in a blue haze beyond the carpet of bog-cotton that smothers the Moss like a field of white poppies, and unsecretive cuckoos chime from the birch trees in the middle distance.

Birch woods rim the Moss and cloak the gentle slope that delineates it from the fields; the ancient build-up of peat and the high water table have raised the surface of the Moss about thirty feet above the fields. Brown hares move effortlessly between the two worlds (the firm, flat Lowland fields, the malevolent uncertainties of the watery, yielding Moss). When the fields are transformed with new grass in early May, the hares' presence is blatant. In the sodden, heathery birch woods, they are as inconspicuous as woodcocks in winter bracken.

* * *

It had been a wet and weary start to May and the Moss seeped water into every surface cavity and hollow, and made mud slicks of deer trails through the birches. Hidden and blatant treacheries awaited every footfall, pools of unguessable depths, God knows how many variations on the theme of sphagnum moss, miraculously concealed and duplicitous patchworks of ground cover that alternated almost firm footing with knee-deep, mud-sucking torture chambers every square yard – unless you are a roe deer, a fox, a pine marten or a brown hare, which travel light and know the ground and all the sure-footed ways through it. The trees want to turn the Moss into a birch wood. The Moss wants to reclaim the wood and fights back with water and ooze. It is a national nature reserve and the management policy consists largely of repelling the birches' advances, stifling old drains, generally giving the bog its head. Still, I am a quiet admirer of the fringing woods and so are the hares.

On a day of merciful respite from a week of rain the sun stirred and steamed the woods with sudden wonderful warmth. I followed my preferred path into the trees, paused by my preferred tree where my habitual leaning presence has begun to wear away lichens from the bark, and bark from the tree. I listened to the day: cuckoo, yellowhammer, willow warblers (dozens of these), wrens (likewise), common gulls (there are three nests on a tiny lochan half a mile across the Moss), swifts (the year's first, I waved a greeting), skylarks (my good omen bird, I smiled). I had been trying to pin down the redstarts for a couple of weeks. I knew there were two pairs, saw one of them mating one afternoon just before the week of rain, and now I could hear the male's distinctive contact call and tried whistling it back to him, but he kept his distance. So I walked on to where the wood became more open, the trees more stunted, the ground more sodden, the going more glutinous.

New movement, not fifty yards ahead, low to the ground among the dark clusters of heather, elusive movement, barely movement at all. Finally there was a blur of dark brown sodden fur between two clumps of heather, but then it stopped dead still. It could be anything at all. The hare is a shape-shifter. If it is lying down with its ears flattened along its spine, it can look like nothing at all. The hare knows this and is accomplished at not being seen. In terrain like this, you can pass two yards from one and never know it's there.

The anything-at-all trembled. The shape shifted. It became taller, developed ears, extraordinary brown and white and grey and black ears that flicked upright and scanned the wood and tuned into the wind. To watch a hare reveal itself piecemeal as it both changes shape from low-lying horizontal to tall-sitting vertical, and inches back and forward among different clumps of heather and skinny birch trunks, is to bear witness to a kind of sorcery. If you came from a land of no hares at all and this was your first view of one, you would surely be inclined to disbelieve your eyes.

A foot appeared where you might not have expected a foot to appear – at the back of one of its ears. That ear – but only that ear – responded to the summons of the foot and lay flat again, but whereas before it had lain flat along the spine, it now flopped forward over its head while the foot groomed it. Grooming over, foot and ear resumed their normal positions, in as much as there is anything at all normal about a brown hare's physiognomy. Then another foot appeared behind the other ear…

The grooming ritual of a brown hare is a time-consuming phenomenon, a kind of stationary ballet characterised by the unlikeliest of body positions devised by a particularly sadistic choreographer. It is all the more surreal and baffling when you can only see about a third of the animal at any one time. But at last the thing was done and the hare eased forward from its sitting-tall pose so that its weight fell forward onto its front feet. At that point there seemed to be so much power folded away and unusable in the back legs and so little available to the too-short front legs (the thought occurs: nature's idea of a tractor) that there was no prospect of forward motion. But the front legs dug in, the back end lifted off the ground, and that created enough space for the back legs to unfold and go to work. They reached forward so far that the rear feet touched down well beyond the front feet, and suddenly the beast was up and running. It turned out that nature knew best all along, as usual.

* * *

A solitary hare travels most of the time with a relaxed gait, whether it is far out in the fields or threading a tortuous capillary-thin route of its own devising through the rain-swollen margins where the birch wood meets the Moss. It was only when that particular hare moved off that I began to catch glimpses of the whole animal between trees and heathery clusters. Its fur was darkened by the sodden vegetation and its legs muddied by the peaty ooze of its track, but in the strong mid-afternoon sunlight the land glittered in a thousand different pockets of standing water from a few inches to a few dozen yards wide. The hare was unflatteringly presented in such uncompromising light but cold fire sprang from its heels, for every footfall produced a splash and every splash was caught and ignited by the sun, and the spectacle was made hypnotic by the soft, rhythmic beat of the hare's stride. Thus it contrived a golden progress across a half a square mile of glaur. As it travelled and became ever more indistinct, vanishing for several seconds at a time, I kept picking it up again because of the sparks that flew from its feet. If I had lived in a time that deified the creatures of the land (and hares were prominent among the earliest of these), what powers might I have ascribed to a creature that crossed the earth on feet of gold?

Some months later, I stumbled across another writer who had recorded precisely the same phenomenon more than 200 years before it had occurred to me – William Wordsworth.

The following is from his lyric poem of 1802, *Resolution and Independence*:

The hare is running races in her mirth;
And with her feet she from the plashy earth
Rasises a mist, that, glittering in the sun,
Runs with her all the way, wherever she doth
run.

* * *

These late spring days seem to be relaxing times for the hares of the Carse. The quiet backroads are defined by hedges and thick grassy verges, linking farms with long straights and sudden right-angle bends. So if I see a hare close enough to the road to make it worthwhile stopping I can rein in my car on the grass verge and briefly use it like a hide, and all the hare sees above the hedge is the windows and the roof. And because it is disinclined to sudden drastic action at such an hour of the day and season of the year, there can be few better circumstances in which to study the creature at ease and in close-up.

Take, for example, that field of what looks to my inexpert eye like it might be kale. There are thousands of plants at regular intervals and in straight rows, each plant about a foot high, and sparse, slender clumps of sweet new grass have moved in to colonise the spaces of bare earth between. Solitary hares are inclined to move in too and to linger while they plunder the grass. Having plundered, they simply linger. The night is the hare's up-and-doing time. An afternoon like this one is often their lying-up time. They like the sun on their backs as much as any other creature. It was in circumstances like these that I started noticing the individuality in hares. That hare we routinely label as "brown" is a patchwork of colours, especially in its summer coat, albeit a patchwork with a limited palette. A hefty specimen was running easily across the field, dead straight towards me, using the rut of a tractor tyre. I guessed female. Like female eagles, the doe outweighs, outmanoeuvres, and (in the hare's case) outboxes the mere males. This one stopped dead about fifty yards from the hedge, and sat back, ears tall. There was no obvious reason for running most of the width of the field, nor for the abrupt stop. There rarely is.

The ears are works of art, and as you rarely see both from the same angle they tend to look mismatched. The left one, which was facing directly towards me, was mostly black, but with two distinct patches of white, one shaped like the tip of a feather, the other like an orchid on a curving stem. The outside edge of the ear was pale gold, such as you might discern in the plumage of a sunlit golden plover. A fern-shaped wisp of tawny clung to the inner edge. From this angle the whole ear was shaped like a feather. The right ear was turned away from me so that all I saw was a narrowed profile, slender at the top, thickening towards the base and curved like the head of a dolphin. What I could see of the fur on the back of the ear was an almost indefinable blending of grey, black and mid-brown, but with the same edge of pale gold as the left ear.

The head was vaguely triangular in profile, but with all the angles rounded. A tiny crew-cut tuft adorned the crown. The head's most noticeable feature was a patch of creamy fur that accommodated the one golden-brown eye I could see, and inclined down towards the black snub nose in two distinct steps. Above and below the cream, the fur lay in dark and light browns, demarcated by vertical lines, one behind and one ahead of the eye. Beneath the nose was white, a shade vividly echoed by the underside of the raised tail (the topside is black). The fur is redder on the back of the head and neck, the lower flanks and the tops of the legs, and the underbelly is a softer, greyer shade of white. The back and upper flanks are predominantly mid-brown, well stippled with black and grey. Such is the palette at the hare's disposal. But no two are identical, and there is no such thing as a brown hare.

The hare in question suddenly noticed something to its left, and took a few paces that way, and in a gesture I have never seen before, lowered and stretched its whole body forward, craning head and neck, scenting something, looking like a stalking cat. That something turned out to be a second hare, flat out and flat-eared and not twenty yards away, the hare that prompted me to stop in the first place. It had registered a twitch of one ear when the newcomer arrived running, but nothing else. The runner had apparently not noticed it until now. The high driving position of my car gave me a much better view of the whole field than the running hare had. I wondered what might happen next. The answer was nothing at all. For all the frantic interaction of boxing hares in late winter and early spring, by and large the hare prefers its own company, and its own space if it is in company. The runner turned and jogged off back across the field, and was still jogging when I lost sight of it.

* * *

A neighbouring field of grass, the early evening of a hot June day, the shade of a road-side oak gave me cover and respite from the sun. Such days are rare events hereabouts. I am inclined to drink them in and marvel at the seductions of being sun-kissed. It was about twenty degrees, which is not really hot unless you were born on the east coast of Scotland, swaddled in the cold breath of the North Sea. I was. So on a day like this one I just want to be out, I just want to marvel, marvel at the sight and the feel of my working territory drenched in equal parts of deep green and gold. And from the shadow of the oak I could see five hares and five curlews and I was content with this, the third and final day of what passes for a heatwave hereabouts.

It occurred to me that the relationship between hares and curlews in this kind of farmland at this time of year must be a familiar one, given how much time they spend within sight and sound of each other, sometimes within touching distance. Yet I cannot remember ever seeing a single moment of interaction between them. There again, they are both instinctively peaceable tribes. But something was going on in the furthest corner of the field. Two of the hares and two of the curlews were over there. One of the other hares was over to my left munching the field edge; another much nearer to me was lying low out in the middle of the field; and the fifth hare was all over the place. It would be tempting to anthropomorphise him as a troublemaker, but only if you are tempted by anthropomorphism in the first place, so let's not be tempted. But he (he looked slighter than the hefty doe in the middle of the field) was up to something. He had just run an improbable distance towards her. I could hear his feet beat the sun-baked earth. He stopped dead. She did not react other than with her ears. He turned and ran but this time on a trajectory that was aimed at the far corner. Halfway there, he stopped and looked back. She had not moved. He turned and resumed his run. Had he been trying to recruit her in the service of whatever point of hare principle was involved in the corner, where something was going on?

Specifically, the two hares already there were involved in what looked from this distance like a skittish schottische, with the apparently accidental consequence that the two curlews preoccupied with deep-underground mining for grubs were suddenly in the centre of the dance floor. Neither bird flinched and neither hare acknowledged their presence or the obstacles they presented. Moments before the fifth hare would have gatecrashed whatever it was that was going on there (and again my guess is that coincidence rather than strategy was at work), the air reverberated with the bittersweet adagio of a small chamber orchestra of curlews that floated down out of the blazing west on stiffly held, down-curved wings, and parked with stately discipline on the hares' dance floor.

The hares stopped dancing. One vanished into long grass, the other began a leisurely stroll along the field edge and in the opposite direction. The curlews were in sole possession of the dance floor, and where there had been two there were now thirty. Just as they settled and fell silent the fifth hare arrived, running. He surged past the outliers of the flock as if they weren't there. The curlews behaved as if the hare wasn't there. He ran through the middle of the flock, swerving round the densest group and bounded on towards the long grass beyond. That's when I noticed the buzzard on the fencepost a little to the right of the curlews.

It slid from the post on wide, unbeating wings and surged forward a yard above the ground towards the running hare. The effect was electric. First, the air was full of curlew wings and curlew cries. Second, if I thought the hare had been running flat out before, I was about to be re-educated, for he swerved left in the corner and began to run back up the field edge, putting as much distance as possible between himself and the bird mayhem in the shortest possible time. This, I now realised, was the first time I had seen a brown hare in full flight. I was frankly sceptical of various claims I had read that they can run at forty-five miles per hour. I am now happy to withdraw my scepticism.

The thing I didn't understand at the time, and still don't, was the buzzard's behaviour. An adult hare is a hopelessly ambitious prey for a buzzard, which is happier with young rabbits and smaller mammals. Was it making mischief after an hour of idleness on a fencepost? Did it think that it might trap the hare in the corner, or the hare might be injured trying to extricate itself? If so, it had misjudged both the hare and the situation, for its immediate airspace was suddenly crowded and fankled by curlew wings and curlew sabres, and deaved by curlew voices, in the face of which it effected a graceless retreat. I am still no wiser about the nature of the relationship between brown hares and curlews, but I am fairly clear that neither species much cares for buzzards.

I turned my attention back to the low-lying hare in the middle of the field, but she was no longer there and in my preoccupation with events in the far corner I had not seen her go. Not seeing hares go is something of a recurring theme for hare-watchers. Then quite suddenly, with my head full of hares and curlews and the miraculous nature of such a day, I was assailed by the memory of an old summer, not in the fields of Stirlingshire leaning on a benevolent oak tree, but on the east coast of the Isle of Skye, watching from a hotel window streaked and strafed and pummelled by the kind of rain in which the island specialises…

THREE

THE RAIN-POLISHED ROAD below and the rain-dulled foreshore of Broadford Bay were all that the evening had left in clear focus. I know this shore. Over there should have been Beinn na Cailleach, out there the mountains of Applecross, the Crowlins, and the steep, blunt stern of Scalpay, but there was only the sea-scudding rain, drifting and dragging opaque grey curtains down from the blurred headlands to whitened wavetops. Pabay was closer in, so a slightly harder-edged and low-slung island profile was visible, a stuttering frieze of trees on its low summit like a comb with missing teeth. I opened the window wide, the better to find something to focus on in what was left of the landscape. Skye does this sometimes, wraps itself in a sodden cocoon of shrouds, sometimes for days, sometimes weeks. The natives know the trick of turning their backs on it and averting their eyes from its grim mesmerism, and so get on with the day's tasks, and it gives them something to complain about in the bar. I have never learned the trick. My work, my day's tasks, lie in the landscape, and Skye's is among the most compelling I know. My eyes drifted, trying to fathom the unfathomable grey. Then a focal point stomped into view from behind the leafy bulk of a sycamore in a shoreline garden.

A low-tide acreage of mud and sand and islets cut off the street from the sea, the preferred realm of a pair of shelduck, a swan-goose kind of creature daubed in handsome technicolour. The basic bodily white is adorned with a dark green head, a chestnut-brown swirl that lies like a halter on back and breast then bisects the belly from breast to tail. There is more brown, and black and blue-black in the secondary wing feathers, and the whole effect is rendered absurd by a scarlet bill (complete with scarlet cherry on the drake) and pink legs and feet. You mistake a shelduck for absolutely nothing else. Some parts of the foreshore were wetter than others, so the birds' reflections came and went as they crossed wetter and drier ground, each set of reflected patterns reshaping fluidly as each bird craned low to feed or stood erect or marched on. In half an hour the shelduck explored the limitless feeding of low tide while the weather began to ease up and a white flare began to burn above Beinn na Cailleach, or rather where Beinn na Cailleach should have been. A pallor of well-watered sunlight-whitened puddles and tidal pools and a rainbow leaped across the east, sizzling down into the sea off Pabay.

My attention wandered to the tiny tidal island of Glas Eilean, its surface thick with grass and nesting common gulls. A kind of organic rhythm characterised the evening. I tuned in slowly, this being my first evening back on the island after a year of missing it from afar. Its pulse was the mud-slapping shelduck, the rainwater swish of occasional passing traffic on the road, the patter of rain, the voices and splashing footfalls of the hotel's early evening clients, the lament of gulls, the staccato chatter of oystercatchers. Then something stirred at the edge of the road, a new movement, a cautious counter-measure to the rhythm, a cat-or-small-dog-sized presence which was palpably neither of these even before I could get a clear view. The rhythm was wrong for one thing, and so were the ears. It was a brown hare. It crossed the road, the hotel car park, and paused on the car park's seaward edge beside the rear wheels of a white van. The ground behind the hotel, a hillside of croft and field and moor, was ideal hare habitat, but the shore, to my un-hare-like brain, seemed to offer slim pickings, and given the added hazards of the road and the to-and-fro of hotel business, I was simply baffled.

A voice called a farewell from the bar door beneath the window, and new footsteps splashed across the road to the car park, white van man returning to claim his white van. He had not seen the hare by his rear wheels. The hare gave no hint that it had seen white van man. It shifted a yard from the back of the van, paused to draw a front paw across an ear. The engine fired and a cloud of diesel fumes belched towards the hare, or rather towards where the hare was a moment earlier. But at the first syllable of the engine it jumped down from the car park on to the shore and headed out across the mud at a run. There were two immediate obstacles – the shelduck. A yard from the first bird it swerved right, only to put itself on a collision course with the second, which it avoided with a four-footed skip to the left.

Back on course, it headed out to Glas Eilean at the same pacy run while the shelduck drew themselves up tall and both turned green and scarlet heads to follow the hare with resigned eyes. Perhaps they knew each other. The van reversed, blocking my view of the hare for several seconds and when its bulk and its stoor and its noise had vanished, so had the hare.

An hour later I closed my writing pad, and, well happed against the weather, I followed the tracks of the hare. That four-footed skip to avoid the second shelduck was as legible in the mud as graffiti on a bus shelter. Thereafter the trail led dead straight to the island where it vanished. There were still nesting gulls there so I declined to linger. There was no sign of the hare and no obvious reason why the island habitat should be worth the risk. I asked around in the hotel. It seems everyone knows the hare and its forays to the island. It has even been known to swim back.

FOUR

IN THE MOUNTAINS the best winter days are the best days of all. Glencoe, a Tuesday in February, a good forecast, an early start, a solo amble through morning mist in the Lairig Eilde, red deer gleaming in the sun as I stepped up out of the mist, clarity and crampons on the Beinn Fhada ridge. I watched a raven fly the entire length of the Lairig. No yard of the floor of the pass was visible, for the mist lay all along the length of its trough. As the bird neared the watershed it entered the sunlight, a glistening piece of jet. Its shadow lagged a few yards behind. Bird and shadow met on a rock of Stob Dubh, and the bird's call was the only sound in the world. A covey of ptarmigan heard my boots bite the snow and spun out over the void of Coire Gabhail, a scatter-gun fusillade of birds. I watched them pitch on snowy screes and disappear in the instant, one of nature's best tricks. Ptarmigan make me smile.

I needed a touch of axemanship to help with a tricky patch on Stob Coire Sgreamhach where the snow had iced up. I climbed on perfect snow in perfect weather on a perfect mountain. Then all that was left was a still and sunlit hands-in-pockets dawdle up the ridge of Bidean nam Bian to a silent, windless summit. No, that was not quite all.

There was a well-worn groove of weekend bootsteps all the way up the ridge, keeping well away from the edge where a fat blue cornice licked out at the mountain air. But mine were not the first footsteps to imprint the snow that morning. Between the weekend climbers' trail and the edge of the cornice was the unmistakable and unmistakably fresh track of a mountain hare. But what on earth was it doing here, running steadily uphill, and so contemptuous from time to time of the cornice edge that I wondered if a mountain hare had ever gone through a cornice and become one of the mountain's unlikelier victims? What kind of mission was it on that led towards the summit of Bidean nam Bian at 3,766 feet? And given that there was no sign of its returning tracks, its most likely onward route from the summit was down the other side, so two miles of ridge-running on frozen snow with not a bite of food, and in such conditions, a brilliantly spotlit moving target for the neighbouring eagles and with nothing remotely resembling an escape route into deep cover, no protection other than its winter whiteness on a winter mountain.

I wondered how it had joined the ridge, for there had been no sign of its tracks on Beinn Fhada. I wondered how far behind I was, and whether I would bump into it on the summit, scratching its head in bemusement, faced with the choice of Bidean's north-west ridge, or the 1,000-foot drop onto the beal-lach followed by a climb almost as high to the summit of Stob Coire an Lochain and a giddy descent down one of its two ridges, each of which ends in one of the Three Sisters of Glencoe, from where there is still the small matter of the rocky descent into the glen. Or else it could hurtle down the snow slopes from the Bidean–Stob Coire beallach into Coire Gabhail, which would be the route of my glissading descent. Or it could go back down the way it had climbed. Mountain hare and brown hare share many characteristics, and one of them is a freedom from logic, or at least from logic as it is defined by a two-legged nature writer.

But I never caught up with the White Hare of Bidean nam Bian, never solved the riddle of what it was doing there, and I have now accorded it mythical status after the fashion of the Grey Man of Beinn MacDhui.

FIVE

THE WIND IS DRY ICE, the sky is pewter-grey and heavily pregnant with unborn snow. The dusk thickens too fast amid the old drifts that patch the hillside. There is that edge of unease about the moment that stems from knowing I am running out of time before darkness falls or snow falls or both fall, and the distance to the road is a mile more than I would like it to be in the circumstances.

But the gloaming is my favourite hour in a situation like this, and my long stillness in the lee of a rock that wears a rakishly canted Glengarry of frozen snow has just offered up the first hint of a reward. A golden eagle has just dropped over the skyline from a leisurely and level exploration of this portion of the broad-backed ridge where I sit, and I have a hunch she might be back.

Why? Because I am as sure as I can be that somewhere up there on the nearest of the old snowfields there are at least two mountain hares. I saw them step from heather on to snow, then the eagle caught my eye and when I tried to find the hares again I couldn't, but I am as sure as I can be that they are still somewhere on the snow, and the eagle's lingering presence may have something to do with that. As the hares see it, there is no point in having a winter-white coat and standing upright among the tussocks like a newly painted milestone when there is an eagle in your portion of the sky. So I submerge the nagging matter of my own travel logistics and command my eyes to see deeper into the shallow white contours above me.

This is among the very oldest stand-offs in the Highlands, the mountain hare and the golden eagle, for both are among the very earliest presences in the landscape, the one the favourite prey of the other, the one trying to outwit the other with stillness and sheer nerve, while the most accomplished pair of wings and the best seeing eyes in my portion of the wild world conspire in a single, simple purpose: to see through the stillness and terrify the hare into reckless panic.

I scoured the old snow, wishing I had eagle eyes so that I knew what the eagle was looking for, how to isolate the different texture and the different shade and quality of hare whiteness from snow whiteness. There again, if the hares are hunkered down behind that shallow fold that runs diagonally across the snow from top right to bottom left, I won't be seeing them unless they move. The eagle, on the other hand, has just sidled back over the skyline as slow as a slug, and begins to head towards the upward edge of the snow. She flies on still wings a yard above the ground. Does she see them yet? Or is she counting on the very menace of her presence to persuade the hares to betray themselves?

Then there is a moment in which her flight is aligned directly with my rock, and apparently looking straight at me and flying at an altitude that could bring her talons into direct contact with me about halfway up my head. Common sense tells me it won't happen, but there is that moment when I borrow briefly from the mountain hare's ancient awareness of itself as an eagle's quarry. I swallow it down and practise hare stillness. The eagle banks sideways a hundred yards away. I am not dressed in mountain hare white and even in my hill-coloured stillness she sees me for what I am and wants no part of it. She wheels uphill on two wingbeats and re-crosses the skyline. If she returns, it will be when I have gone. Something like twenty winters ago and on this same hill, I saw more than thirty mountain hares explode from an old snowfield in similar circumstances, an eagle leaning against the wind. Now I see two and that's two more than I see most days when I'm in what should still be mountain hare country.

Something tells me my time is up. That was my moment; no denouement, but so beautiful in its setting and its suppressed tension that I feel fulfilled by it. I rise and turn away downhill, and turn my face to the sky in a wordless "thank you" to who knows what. A single snowflake blinks into an eye. Another trembles on the back of my glove.

AFTERWORD

The brown hare (*Lepus europaeus*) and the mountain hare (*Lepus timidus*) are lagomorphs, a biological tribe that includes rabbits. The brown hare is widespread through Britain and much of mainland Europe, but it is essentially a Lowlander. The mountain hare, variously known as the blue hare and the white hare (wisely named in French *le lièvre variable*), is a Highlander. Most of its British population lives on the high ground of the Scottish Highlands and Borders, although it will come to lower levels in extreme winter weather when too much snow obliterates its food sources. It is also found in Ireland (where it does not change colour), in Iceland and in Scandinavia. In North America, its close cousin, the snowshoe rabbit, is a hare in all but name. The American nature writer Ernest Thompson Seton wrote in *Wild Animals at Home* (Doubleday, New York, 1913) that "the snowshoe rabbit is a cross between a rabbit and a snowdrift"; I wish I'd thought of that.

Everyone knows at least two things about the hare – it boxes in the early spring (hence 'mad March hare') something like a miniature kangaroo, and it comes in a distant second to the tortoise in Aesop's fable. The first of these is the centrepiece of mating rituals, when a doe (also known as a jill, for no good reason) is pursued around a field by a mob of bucks (also known as – you've guessed it – jacks).

These giddy episodes are often ignited by the doe, and she will, from time to time, get up on her hind legs and flail her front feet at the nearest buck, in the manner of a sparring boxer. It is ritual and bluff rather than a fight. When a hare wants to inflict injury it doesn't use its "fists". It kicks, using its back legs to unforgettable effect (see Chapter One). The mating ritual usually kicks off in February, and it is over the next few months that hares are at their most visible during the daylight hours.

Aesop's yarn, on the other hand, seems to be making a point about the hare's unwillingness to run straight from A to B without being distracted, as well as counselling life's plodders to keep on plodding on the off-chance that plodding sometimes achieves spectacular results.

But hares also lay claim to two of nature's more unusual characteristics – refection and superfoetation. Refection is a practice designed to improve digestive efficiency by recycling the cellulose in their diet. To put it bluntly, and there really is no other way to put it, they eat their own droppings. Superfoetation means becoming pregnant while pregnant. Don't try this at home.

Our relationship with the hare is ancient and complex. It is a notable component in stories and rituals of witchcraft – the witch becoming hare, the hare becoming witch, that kind of thing. One skittish twist in that cycle of events maintained that if the witch was injured during her hare phase she would show the identical injury when she was restored to her witchiness.

The hare has also been a favourite subject of artists since the earliest cave painters (and, famously, of Albrecht Dürer), and of writers at least since the ancient Greeks. Look in any populist art gallery today and you will see dozens of drawings, paintings, etchings, woodcuts, sculptures and jewellery pieces that depict hares. (If it is a particularly good gallery, it might feature the work of Carry Akroyd, as displayed on the cover of this book.)

Yet all that admiration, inspiration and superstition is but one side of the two-sided nature of our relationship with hares. The other is a tendency to want to kill them in large numbers, whether by "coursing" – killing them with dogs, for the hell of it – or shooting them in organised "drives". It took Robert Burns to unite those two facets of the relationship. In a letter of April 1789 he wrote that "while sowing in the fields, I heard a shot, and presently a poor little hare limped by me, apparently very much hurt … this set my humanity in tears".

The result was the majestically titled poem, *Verses On Seeing a Wounded Hare Limp By Me, Which a Fellow Had Just Shot At*:

Hare

INHUMAN man! curse on thy barbarous art,
And blasted be thy murder-aiming eye;
May never pity soothe thee with a sigh
Nor ever pleasure glad thy cruel heart!

Go, live, poor wanderer of the wood and field!
The bitter little that of life remains:
No more the thickening brakes and verdant plains
To thee shall home, or food, or pastime yield.

Seek, mangled wretch, some place of wonted rest,
No more of rest, but now thy dying bed!
The sheltering rushes whistling o'er thy head,
The cold earth with thy bloody bosom prest.

Oft as by the winding Nith, I musing, wait
The sober eve, or hail the cheerful dawn;
I'll miss thee sporting o'er the dewy lawn,
And curse the ruffian's aim, and mourn thy hapless fate.

Well over 200 years later, inhuman man's barbarous art still delights in blasting the poor wanderer of the wood and field, and its fate is no less hapless. How bad has it got? We know from a British government committee report in 1996 that at the turn of the twentieth century there were an estimated four million brown hares in Britain, and that in the next 100 years its numbers declined by eighty per cent. They haven't all been shot, of course, or maimed by dogs. The most ruthless of our inventions in terms of the toll it takes on hares is the internal combustion engine. The fact that the remains of hares turn up so often in fox dens is because of the ready availability of road kills. The decline is also due to changed agricultural practices, especially the change from hay to silage, and the decline, over much of its chosen landscape, of a year-round supply of food for an animal that neither hibernates nor stores body fat.

The mountain hare has the distinction of being perhaps the favourite prey of golden eagles, and as our population of white-tailed eagles grows and expands its range, they are becoming a noticeable presence in areas favoured by mountain hares. But the toll eagles take is paltry compared to the culling of sporting estates.

Questions were even asked in the Scottish Parliament in 2014 about culling mountain hares. The answers were not all that one might have hoped for. In summary, the reasons mountain hares are shot are for tick control (yet another manifestation of the obsessive management of grouse moors), for "sporting purposes" (killing for the sake of killing, and killing to make money; we don't eat hare in twenty-first-century Scotland, but Italians have been known to fill refrigerated vans with Scottish mountain hares and take them home). And mountain hares are also snared, said the Minister, "for the protection of crops or forests". The mountain hare as a feller of forests takes some swallowing.

Then there is the question of numbers. No one knows how many are shot each year, although in 2006 a Scottish Natural Heritage report on the control of mountain hares on Scottish estates produced a figure of 24,529.

Worse, no one knows how many mountain hares there are. The only officially published information was that 1996 study, when an estimate of 350,000 was "subject to a fifty per cent margin of error".

The arithmetic is grim. Twenty years ago, the population could have been as low as 175,000, and if the 2006 cull was anything like average and the estates have been taking out 25,000 each year, then the mountain hare is on the wrong side of an irresistible momentum and the estates' determination to "manage" accounts for a steep descent towards its extinction. A study by the *Journal of Applied Ecology* in 2009 concluded that "there is no compelling evidence that culling hares might increase red grouse density".

On the other hand, the RSPB points out that golden eagles prey on mountain hares and hen harriers prey on leverets, and you would think it would be in the interests of grouse moor managers to ensure that there was something else other than grouse for predators to eat. But then this is an industry that is so paranoid about ticks that it has taken to putting out boxes of medicated grit for grouse to ingest, so logic does not appear to be its strong suit either. The mountain hare, as an occasionally inconvenient presence for a particular form of human land use, is simply the latest visible symptom of a phenomenon that has been going on since our ancestors eradicated the wolf.

* * *

There is a no-man's land for our two species of hare. It lies where Highlands meet Lowlands, for example in the high fields of north Angus a few miles inland from Scotland's east coast, and north of the Tay estuary. The mountain hare still maintains something like a stronghold in those beefy, rounded hills above the Blackwater reservoir between Glen Isla and Glen Prosen. This is my calf country, the destination of many family excursions in childhood, and later the first of all my solo hill-walking landscapes. These, and the couthier Sidlaw Hills to the south of Strathmore were (and, in my mind, they still remain) my hills of home, and in time they would become a bridge to the Cairngorms in the longed-for north. I feel as if all this should have an ancient Pictish name that translates into The Land of the Two Hares.

Came the winter, and a sullen succession of north-easterlies fleeced the hills in luxurious depths of snow. Then the wind fell away, high pressure set in, and that white land froze for weeks. It is at times like these that mountain hares will yield temporarily to the unequal struggle to make ends meet. So they descend to the lower ground below the snow line where, comparatively speaking, the land is quiet and mild and grey-green. That winter, from Angus and the Cairngorms all the way west to Glencoe, the high hills were horizontally bisected by an alpine snow line. Old mountaineering sages swore they had never seen so much snow high up. But on the low ground, the natives basked in the most tranquil of winters, and wherever they had views to the mountains they shook their wondering heads and marvelled.

I was up along the Isla on a beaver ploy, and afterwards wandered up towards the snow line. On a quiet road between the highest fields and the snow I stopped to watch a brown hare feeding along the top edge of a rough grassy bank that rose above a small burn. There are certain circumstances of winter when the higher margins of cultivated land are more productive, from the hare's way of looking at things, than the exhausted fertility of the Lowlands.

Over a quarter of an hour the hare edged slowly uphill until it was within a hundred yards of the snow. At that moment a small lump of snow broke loose from the hillside and slid down towards the hare and the bank. The hare started, and stared at it for fully ten seconds, then turned its back and resumed its more pressing quest of finding food. As I watched it slide, the lump of snow metamorphosed into a mountain hare in full midwinter regalia. Against the snow, I simply hadn't seen it, but now that it was in among the rough grass and sparse heather, it was suddenly as vivid as a lighthouse.

So I swung the binoculars slowly along the lowest snow slope and found four more mountain hares, two just above and two just below the edge of the snow.

And then I had what Ernest Hemingway called "one of those unsound but illuminating thoughts". On how many hillsides the length and breadth of the Highlands that extraordinary winter was this phenomenon being enacted, where the particular nature of the snowfall had lured both mountain hares and brown hares to the same shallow contour just below the comfort zone of one and just above the comfort zone of the other, there to eke out a few days or a few weeks of meagre sustenance? And yet, it is characteristic of the determinedly independent, solitary nature of these endlessly intriguing and beguiling animals that for both tribes the presence of the other was unsurprising, a thing of cool indifference.

For me it was a moment of quietly satisfying discovery. But then I fancied I could hear the far-off echo of some wandering Pictish scribe of these same lands from their heyday a thousand years removed from mine: "You took an awful long time to work that one out."

The Hare Preservation Trust works to gain legal protection for hares during the breeding season; raise awareness of threats to hares, particularly illegal hunting; support research into the reason for the hares decline; provide information for the public when they find injured or abandoned hares; and to act as a focal point for hare information.

Nature Writing by Jim Crumley

Symphonic
Watching Wildlife
Seasons of Storm and Wonder
Lakeland Wild
The Nature of Spring
The Nature of Winter
The Nature of Autumn
Nature's Architect
The Eagle's Way
The Great Wood
The Last Wolf
The Winter Whale
Brother Nature
Something Out There
A High and Lonely Place
The Company of Swans
Gulfs of Blue Air
The Heart of the Cairngorms
The Heart of Mull
The Heart of Skye
Among Mountains
Among Islands
Badgers on the Highland Edge
Waters of the Wild Swan
The Pentland Hills
Shetland – Land of the Ocean
Glencoe – Monarch of Glens
West Highland Landscape
St Kilda

Jim Crumley is a nature writer, journalist, poet, and passionate advocate for our wildlife and wild places. He is the author of more than forty books, and is a newspaper and magazine columnist and an occasional broadcaster on both BBC radio and television.

He has written in depth on topics as diverse as beavers, eagles, wolves, whales, native woods, mountains, seasons, climate change and species reintroductions. He has also written companions to this volume on the barn owl, swan and badger.